JUNE 04

Education and Training in Forensic Science

A Guide for Forensic Science Laboratories, Educational Institutions, and Students

Developed and Approved by the Technical Working Group for Education and Training in Forensic Science

NCJ 203099

Sarah V. Hart
Director

The National Institute of Justice is a component of the Office of Justice Programs, which also includes the Bureau of Justice Assistance, the Bureau of Justice Statistics, the Office of Juvenile Justice and Delinquency Prevention, and the Office for Victims of Crime.

Message From the Director

Forensic scientists play a pivotal role in the criminal justice system, providing crucial information about the evidence to the trier of fact. Because the work they do both at the crime scene and in the laboratory often must be used in court, it is especially important that the training and education of forensic scientists provide a solid scientific background and a broad base in criminalistics.

Interest in forensic science has increased dramatically in the past 10 years. In response to this interest, many universities have begun to offer degrees in forensic science at both the undergraduate and graduate level. To ensure that these programs adequately prepare practitioners for their careers in operational laboratories, the U.S. Department of Justice (DOJ) has supported West Virginia University's establishment of the Technical Working Group for Education and Training in Forensic Science for the purpose of recommending best practices for educational curriculums in forensic science. These recommendations encompass the current best practices and procedures for initial and continuing training models to provide those seeking to become forensic scientists with the educational and practical knowledge and skills necessary to effectively support their role in the criminal justice system.

This publication is especially timely as President Bush has directed DOJ to undertake a $1 billion, 5-year program to improve the Nation's capacity to use DNA evidence as a routine law enforcement tool. This capacity-building plan seeks to improve all aspects of the system—evidence collection, presentation, analysis, and use in court. Ensuring that this Nation has an adequate pool of trained forensic scientists is critical to achieving this goal.

I commend the hard work of the members of the Technical Working Group that created this consensus document. They are representative of forensic science educators, laboratory directors, forensic science trainers, education professionals, prosecutors, and defense attorneys. Their collective expert knowledge, experience, and dedication to the task made this effort a success.

Educational programs and training models will vary based on the needs of the particular organization and jurisdiction in which they are implemented. The criteria set forth in this document can serve as a guide for universities to promote quality education and training in forensic science disciplines by promoting a consistent approach while tailoring their programs to meet the needs of the applicable community.

Sarah V. Hart
Director,
National Institute of Justice

Technical Working Group on Education and Training in Forensic Science

The Technical Working Group on Education and Training in Forensic Science (TWGED) is a multidisciplinary group of content area experts from across the United States and Canada, from both urban and rural jurisdictions, each representing his or her respective agency or practice. Each individual is involved in educating and/or training forensic scientists (as students or professionals). They represent academia, forensic science laboratories, professional forensic science organizations, and the legal system.

At the outset of the effort to develop this *Guide,* the National Institute of Justice (NIJ) created a planning panel—composed of forensic science educators, crime laboratory directors, and trainers—to define needs, develop initial strategies, and steer the larger group. This planning panel first determined that an NIJ technical working group would provide the best approach for addressing the demonstrated needs. Additional members of the technical working group were then selected from recommendations solicited from the planning panel and national organizations, including the American Academy of Forensic Sciences, American Society of Crime Laboratory Directors, American Society of Crime Laboratory Directors/Laboratory Accreditation Board, International Association for Identification, Drug Enforcement Administration, Federal Bureau of Investigation, George Washington University, West Virginia University, Marshall University, and the National Forensic Science Technology Center.

During a 1-year period, the 47 members and 2 designees of the TWGED listed below worked together to develop this *Guide*:

Education and Training in Forensic Science Planning Panel

Dr. Jack Ballantyne
Associate Professor
Department of Chemistry
University of Central Florida
Orlando, FL

Inspector Mark Dale
Laboratory Director
New York State Police
Albany, NY

Dr. Allison Eastman
Supervisor of DNA Services
New York State Police
Albany, NY

Linda Errichetto
Laboratory Director
Las Vegas Metropolitan Police Department Forensic Laboratory
Las Vegas, NV

Dr. Terry Fenger
Director
Marshall University Forensic Science Center
Huntington, WV

Barry Fisher
Director
Scientific Services Bureau
Los Angeles County Sheriff's Office
Los Angeles, CA

Dr. Jane Homeyer
Forensic Science Training Unit Chief
Laboratory Division
Federal Bureau of Investigation
Quantico, VA

Peter Marone
Central Lab Director
Division of Forensic Sciences
Commonwealth of Virginia
Richmond, VA

Dr. Carl Selavka
Director
Massachusetts State Police Crime Laboratory
Sudbury, MA

Dr. Ian Tebbett
Education and Training Consultant
University of Florida
Gainesville, FL

Dr. Michael Yura
Director
Forensic Identification Program
West Virginia University
Morgantown, WV

Additional Technical Working Group Members

Dr. José Almirall
Director
Forensic Science Program
Florida International University
Miami, FL

Kathleen Barch
Deputy Director
Ohio Bureau of Criminal Identification and Investigation
London, OH

Dr. Clifton Bishop
Curriculum Coordinator and Advisor
Forensic Identification Program
West Virginia University
Morgantown, WV

Garry Bombard
Director of Training
Illinois State Police Department
Forensic Sciences Command
Chicago, IL

Dr. Robert Briner
Director
Southeast Missouri Regional Crime Laboratory
Cape Girardeau, MO

Dr. Michael Bourke
DNA Manager
Connecticut Department of Public Safety
Meriden, CT*

Dr. Yale Caplan
Director
National Scientific Services
Baltimore, MD

Elizabeth Carpenter
Laboratory Director
Oregon State Police Crime Laboratory
Portland, OR

Alan Clark
Associate Deputy Assistant Administrator
Office of Forensic Sciences
Drug Enforcement Agency Headquarters
Washington, DC

Dr. Peter DeForest
Professor of Criminalistics
John Jay College
City University of New York
New York, NY

Dr. Christopher D'Elia
Vice President for Research
State University of New York
Albany, NY

Dr. Jamie Downs
Director/Chief Medical Examiner
Alabama Department of Forensic Sciences
Auburn, AL

Dr. David Foran
Assistant Professor
George Washington University
Department of Forensic Sciences
Washington, DC

Dr. James Fox
Lipman Family Professor of Criminal Justice
College of Criminal Justice
Northeastern University
Boston, MA

Dr. Robert Fraas
Director
Forensic Science Program
Eastern Kentucky University
Richmond, KY

Dr. Robert Gaensslen
Director of Graduate Studies
Forensic Science Program
University of Illinois at Chicago
Chicago, IL

Dr. Howard Harris
Director
Forensic Science Program
University of New Haven
West Haven, CT

Dr. Neal Haskell
Forensic Entomologist
St. Joseph's College
Rensselaer, IN

Carol Henderson, J.D.
Professor of Law
Shepard Broad Law Center
Nova Southeastern University
Fort Lauderdale, FL

Dwane Hilderbrand
Scottsdale Crime Laboratory
Scottsdale, AZ

Karen Irish
Director of Forensic Sciences
Baltimore County Police Department
Towson, MD

Susan Johns
Bureau Chief
Illinois State Police
Springfield, IL

Dr. Graham Jones
President
Forensic Specialties Accreditation Board
Medical Examiner's Office
Edmonton, Alberta, Canada

Dr. Karen Kershenstein
President
KWK Enterprises
Fairfax Station, VA

Kevin Lothridge
Deputy Director
National Forensic Science and Technology Center
Largo, FL

Joseph Polski
Chief Operations Officer
International Association for Identification
Mendota Heights, MN

Lawrence Presley
Director of Criminalistics
National Medical Services
Willow Grove, PA

Victor Reeve
Laboratory Director
California Criminalistics Institute
Sacramento, CA

Gerald Richards
Richards Forensic Services
Laurel, MD

Dr. Kathy Roberts
Assistant Professor
California State University
Los Angeles, CA

Linda Rourke
John Jay College
City University of New York
Bayside, NY*

Dr. George Sensabaugh
Professor of Biomedical and Forensic Sciences
University of California
Berkeley, CA

Dr. Charles Tindall
Director of Forensic Science
Metropolitan State College of Denver
Denver, CO

Dr. Victor Weedn
Principal Research Scientist and Director of Biotechnology and Health Initiatives
Carnegie Mellon University
Pittsburgh, PA

Dr. Jeffrey Wells
Associate Professor
Department of Justice Sciences
University of Alabama at Birmingham
Birmingham, AL

Wayne Williams, J.D.
Electronic Consultant/Attorney-at-Law
Hyattsville, MD

Amy Wong
Laboratory Director
Virginia Division of Forensic Science
Fairfax, VA

Kenneth Zercie
Assistant Director
Connecticut State Police Forensic Laboratory
Meriden, CT

**Designee who attended one meeting as a proxy for a TWGED member.*

Acknowledgments

The National Institute of Justice (NIJ) and West Virginia University (WVU) wish to thank the members of the Technical Working Group on Education and Training in Forensic Science (TWGED) for their extensive efforts and dedication to the enhancement of education and training in forensic science. The TWGED members, who are national experts representing academia, forensic science laboratories, professional organizations, and the legal system, generously gave their time to draft and review this document. In addition, thanks are extended to the agencies and organizations that TWGED members represent for their flexibility and support, which enabled the participants to see this project to completion.

NIJ and WVU would like to thank all the individuals from various national organizations who responded to the request for nominations of experts with a wide expanse of knowledge and experience from different areas of forensic science, both in practice and education. It was from their recommendations that the members were selected. In particular, thanks to Mary Fran Ernst from the American Academy of Forensic Sciences, Keith K. Coonrod from the American Society of Crime Laboratory Directors, Robert S. Conley from the American Society of Crime Laboratory Directors/Laboratory Accreditation Board, Thomas C. Smith from the American Bar Association, Criminal Justice Section, Jennifer S. Mihalovich from the American Board of Criminalistics, Thomas Janovsky from the Drug Enforcement Agency, Dick Johnson from the National White Collar Crime Center, Dr. Michael Baer from the American Council on Education, Dr. Jay Siegel from Michigan State University, Dr. Ray H. Liu from the University of Alabama–Birmingham, Dr. David A. Rowley from the George Washington University, and Dr. Philip H. Yeagle from the University of New Haven. NIJ, WVU, and TWGED also would like to thank the numerous individuals and organizations who were sent a draft of the *Guide* for review and comment.

WVU would like to thank President David Hardesty, Provost Gerry Lang, Vice President for Research John Weete, Director of the Forensic Identification Program Michael Yura, Forensic Identification Program Administrative Assistant Lori Britton, and Projects Director Max M. Houck for their commitment and dedication to the forensic sciences and this project.

About This Report

The results of forensic investigations often can be the difference between acquittal and conviction in a court of law. The validity of those results depends on the knowledge, skills, and experience of the forensic scientists working to obtain them. The National Institute of Justice, with support from the West Virginia University, created the Technical Working Group for Education and Training in Forensic Science (TWGED) to establish best practices for educating and training forensic scientists. The working group developed the consensus criteria and recommendations presented in this report. This information serves students as they prepare for a career in forensic science, educational institutions as they develop and revamp curriculums, and forensic scientists as they advance their knowledge, skills, and abilities in the constantly evolving forensic science disciplines.

What does the working group recommend?

A solid educational background in natural sciences with extensive laboratory coursework establishes the groundwork for a career in forensic science. Strong personal attributes, professional skills, certification, and professional involvement also are critical to the professional growth of prospective and practicing forensic scientists.

Undergraduate degree. Undergraduate forensic science degree programs are expected to deliver a strong and credible science foundation that emphasizes the scientific method and problem-solving skills. Exemplary programs would be interdisciplinary and include substantial laboratory work, as most employment opportunities occur in laboratory settings. Natural sciences should dominate undergraduate curriculums and be supported by coursework in specialized, forensic, and laboratory sciences and other classes that complement the student's area of concentration.

Graduate degree. Graduate programs can move students from theoretical concepts to discipline-specific knowledge. Exemplary curriculums can include such topics as crime scenes, physical evidence, law/science interface, ethics, and quality assurance to complement the student's advanced coursework. Graduate programs should be designed with strong laboratory and research components. Access to instructional laboratories with research-specific facilities, equipment, and instrumentation and interaction with forensic laboratories are required to enhance the graduate-level experience. By emphasizing written and oral communication and report writing, graduate programs can prepare students for future courtroom testimony.

Forensic scientists have an ongoing obligation to advance their field through training and continuing professional development. Training programs should include written components (e.g., instructor qualifications, student requirements, performance goals, and competency testing), and their content should contain several core and discipline-specific elements guided by peer-defined standards. Continuing professional development—mechanisms through which forensic scientists remain current or advance their expertise—should be structured, measurable, and documented.

Who should read this report?

Forensic science laboratory managers involved with hiring and training forensic scientists, educational institutions that offer or are seeking to establish forensic science programs, and individuals beginning or continuing careers in forensic science.

Contents

Introduction

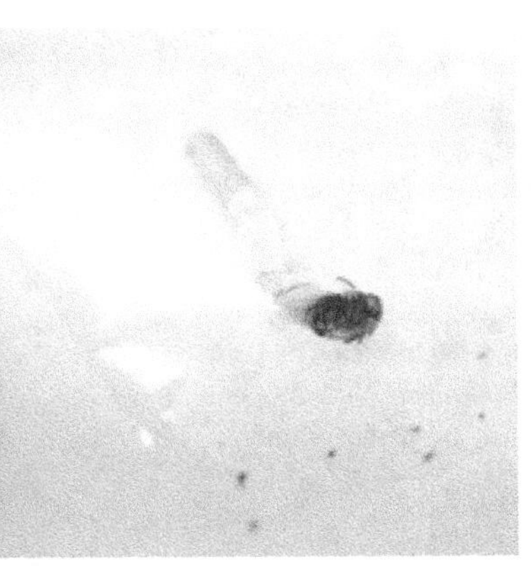

Forensic science plays a crucial role in the justice system by providing scientific and foundational information for investigations and the courts.[1] The Technical Working Group on Education and Training in Forensic Science (TWGED) focused primarily on education and ***training*** in those disciplines traditionally and generally associated with the work of ***forensic science laboratories,*** commonly referred to as ***"criminalistics."*** (For more information on criminalistics, see "What Is 'Criminalistics'?") Criminalistics is the profession and scientific discipline directed toward the recognition, identification, individualization, and evaluation of physical evidence in legal proceedings by the application of the ***natural sciences.*** There are many other forensic science specialty areas whose educational and training requirements are distinctly different from the traditional laboratory science areas, such as forensic computer science, forensic entomology, and forensic psychology; these are more fully described in appendix A.

How to Use This Guide

This *Guide* is intended for use by forensic science laboratories in hiring and training forensic scientists, educational institutions offering or seeking to establish forensic science programs, and individuals beginning or continuing careers in forensic science.

Forensic science laboratories can use this *Guide* in a variety of ways. It offers suggested qualifications for prospective employees' academic background, which may assist laboratories in posting and filling forensic science positions. The *Guide* also provides structure for the continuing education of practicing forensic scientists and training to enhance a current employee's ***knowledge, skills, and abilities (KSAs).***

Educational institutions can use this *Guide* to gauge the curriculum and structure of their forensic science academic programs. As a reflection of the forensic science community's needs and requirements, this *Guide* also may provide direction and ideas for the design or expansion of these programs.

In addition, prospective forensic science students can use this *Guide* to assist them in evaluating forensic science academic programs. It can also provide guidance regarding the requirements, career paths, and expectations for a career in forensic science.

Background

As stated in NIJ's 1999 publication *Forensic Sciences: Review of Status and Needs,* the educational and training needs "of the forensic community are immense. Training of newcomers to the field, as well as providing continuing education for seasoned professionals, is vital to ensuring that crime laboratories deliver the best possible service to the criminal justice system. Forensic scientists must stay up to date as new technology, equipment,

What Is "Criminalistics"?

"Criminalistics is the science and profession dealing with the recognition, collection, identification, individualization, and interpretation of physical evidence, and the application of the natural sciences to law-science matters. The term originated from the book *Handbuch fur Untersuchungsrichter als System der Kriminalististik* (3d ed., 1898) by Hans Gross, an investigating magistrate and professor of criminology at the University of Prague. He described the need for a scientifically trained investigator who could undertake certain technical aspects of an investigation and could also serve as liaison between scientific specialists who might assist in the investigation of criminal activity. This concept was popular in Europe, where a number of forensic science institutes were developed to apply the tools and techniques of the natural sciences to the investigation of crime and, generally, in official governmental inquiries."[a]

The following specialized areas may be included under the criminalistics umbrella: ***biology*** (including biochemistry, molecular biology, and DNA analysis);[b] ***chemistry;*** toxicology; microscopy; analysis of controlled substances, fire debris, explosive residues, hairs, fibers, glass, soil, paint and other materials, and fingerprints and other impressions (such as footwear and tire tracks); questioned documents; toolmark and firearms identification; and reconstruction and reconstruction patterns.

Like other scientific and technical subjects, forensic science and criminalistics have specialized terminology that may not always be clear to nonspecialists. In addition, professionals in the field may not agree on the meaning of every term. To help make this document more accessible, some of the terms used to describe specialized areas of criminalistics are discussed here.

In biological evidence analysis, the term "forensic serology" was common for a long time because blood groups were among the individual features of blood and physiological fluids. "Serology" is the study of blood groups (blood types). In the 1970s, a number of proteins, some of which were enzymes, came into use as additional individual characteristics of blood and physiological fluids, and the term "forensic biochemistry" came into use. With the introduction of DNA typing in the mid-1980s, forensic scientists no longer used blood types, enzymes, or other proteins to characterize biological evidence. The term "forensic molecular biology" tries to capture forensic DNA analysis. "Forensic biology" usually now means the analysis of blood and physiological fluids, including DNA typing. Some specialized areas such as analysis of botanical evidence also are part of "forensic biology."

"Forensic chemistry" sometimes means the use of analytical chemical methods to analyze controlled substances (illegal drugs). It also commonly encompasses the use of chemical methods to analyze fibers, glass, soil, paint, and other materials. These materials have often been called ***trace evidence*** in forensic science, but lately, some professionals have come to recognize that "trace" is a misleading term for this class of evidence. For one thing, it implies that there is a small quantity, which is not necessarily true. Microscopy is commonly used to conduct these types of examinations.

Fingerprint analysis includes automated fingerprint identification system (AFIS) technologies, methods for developing latent fingerprints, and fingerprint comparison and identification. The latter two areas are most often identified with criminalistics.

Toolmark and firearms identification refers to the use of class and individual markings made by tools or firearms to attribute markings to specific tools or bullets and/or cartridge cases to specific weapons.

Questioned documents, sometimes called "forensic document examination," includes several different types of examinations: comparing

handwriting with known handwriting samples to determine whether or not a document was written by a specific individual; examining machine-prepared documents (e.g., typewriting) to determine what type of machine or whether a specific machine was used to prepare the document; analysis of forgeries, counterfeit money, or identification documents; and restoration of damaged or altered documents.

"Reconstruction" uses physical evidence and its analysis to help put together past events in time and/or space. Reconstructions typically require the documentation and analysis of patterns such as bloodstain or glass fracture patterns. Reconstruction as a part of criminalistics usually implies not only studying patterns but also incorporating laboratory-based physical evidence analysis (and at times, analysis of the crime scene) into the final hypothesis.

Note

a. Barnett, P. "Criminalistics," *McGraw-Hill Encyclopedia of Science & Technology*, 9th ed. M. Licker (ed.). New York: McGraw-Hill, Inc., 2002.

b. Words defined in the glossary are set in ***bold/italic type*** on first use to distinguish them from other text.

methods, and techniques are developed. While training programs exist in a variety of forms, there is a need to broaden their scope and build on existing resources."[2]

Forensic Sciences: Review of Status and Needs made a number of recommendations, including seeking mechanisms for—

- Accreditation/***certification*** of forensic academic training programs/institutions.
- Setting national consensus standards of education in the forensic sciences.
- Establishing independent, community-wide, consensus standard-setting bodies, such as Technical Working Groups.
- Funding by NIJ of forensic academic research and development programs.
- Ensuring that all forensic scientists have professional orientations to the field, formal ***quality-assurance*** training, and expert-witness training.

In recent years, the demand for forensic scientists has increased for many reasons, including population demographics, increased awareness of forensic science by law enforcement, increased numbers of law enforcement officers, database automation in several categories of physical evidence, jury expectations, legal requirements, accreditation and certification requirements of laboratories and personnel, impending retirement of a large number of currently practicing forensic scientists, and increased public awareness of forensic science through the popular media. The increased demand places a greater responsibility on educational institutions and the forensic science community to meet this challenge. TWGED was created in response to the needs expressed by the justice system, including the forensic science and law enforcement communities, to establish best practices for training and education in forensic science.

Origin of the Planning Panel and the Technical Working Group

In the summer of 2001, the American Academy of Forensic Sciences (AAFS), the American Society of Crime Laboratory Directors/Laboratory Accreditation Board (ASCLD/LAB), and the American Society of Crime Laboratory Directors (ASCLD) encouraged NIJ and WVU to establish TWGED. NIJ and WVU selected a 10-member planning panel. The members represented forensic science laboratory directors, educators, and trainers. The rationale for their involvement was twofold: They represented the diversity of the professional disciplines and each organization is a key stakeholder in the future of education and training in forensic science.

The planning panel was charged with developing an outline for a guide for education and training in forensic science. The planning panel also was charged with identifying experts to serve as members of TWGED.

Candidates for TWGED were recommended by law enforcement and forensic science organizations and educational programs that educate and train forensic scientists, prosecutors, and defense attorneys. The following criteria were used to select TWGED members:

- Each member was nominated/selected for the position by the planning panel and/or national organizations.
- Each member had specific knowledge in education and/or training in forensic science.
- Each member could commit to the project for at least a 12-month period.

Forty-nine experts (20 forensic science educators and trainers, 22 forensic science laboratory managers, 2 attorneys, and 5 experts from other organizations) from 20 States, the District of Columbia, and 1 Canadian province were invited to be members of the working group. This distribution of expertise brought together all of the necessary resources to produce this *Guide*.

Chronology

The planning panel meeting. In the summer of 2001, the planning panel met in Morgantown, West Virginia, to prepare the project objectives and begin the guide development process. The planning panel's objective was to develop an outline for a guide based on existing programs in forensic science education and current models for forensic science training and present it for review to the assembled TWGED at a later date. During this initial session, the planning panel identified five distinct topics for inclusion in the *Guide,* which were distilled into four final sections.

The *Guide's* content has the following format:

- An *introduction.*
- A section on *model criteria* that sets forth minimum recommendations.
- A section on *implementation* that describes how to execute the recommendations.
- A *summary* that justifies performing the procedures.

TWGED meetings. In November 2001, TWGED met in Morgantown, West Virginia, and in January 2002, it met in San Diego, California. The group was separated into four committees to draft the sections of the *Guide:* Qualifications for a Career in Forensic Science, Undergraduate Curriculum in Forensic Science, Graduate Curriculum in Forensic Science, and Training/Continuing Education in Forensic Science. An editor from Aspen Systems Corporation attended each of the breakout sessions to facilitate the drafting process. When the breakout sections were completed, the full TWGED assembled to evaluate their work.

The planning panel reassembled in San Antonio, Texas, in March 2002 to review comments from the TWG and incorporate them into the *Guide*.

In April 2002, TWGED met in Arlington, Virginia, to review, revise, and complete the initial document. The draft was edited and TWGED members were asked to recommend persons, organizations, or agencies they felt should comment on the draft. This draft was then sent to these stakeholder organizations and to all TWG members. (See appendix B for a list of non-TWGED reviewers.)

Finally, in August 2002, the planning panel met in Las Vegas, Nevada, to review the latest draft, make revisions, and approve changes. In addition, the planning panel reviewed the *Guide's* glossary, title, introduction, a list of forensic science professional and certification organizations (appendix C), and a list of the scientific and technical working groups (appendix D) and any published educational requirements from them (appendix E).

Notes

1. Words defined in the glossary are set in ***bold/italic type*** on first use to distinguish them from other text.

2. National Institute of Justice, *Forensic Sciences: Review of Status and Needs,* Issues and Practices, Washington, DC: U.S. Department of Justice, National Institute of Justice, February 1999, NCJ 173412, p. 4.

Qualifications for a Career in Forensic Science

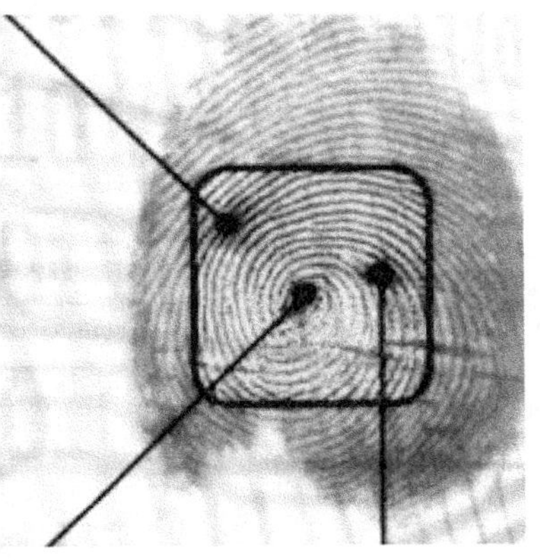

Introduction

Forensic science plays a crucial role in the criminal justice system. As an applied science, it requires a strong foundation in the natural sciences and the development of practical skills in the application of these sciences to a particular discipline. A forensic scientist must be capable of integrating knowledge and skills in the examination, analysis, interpretation, reporting, and testimonial support of physical evidence. A properly designed forensic science program should address these needs and strengthen the student's knowledge, skills, and abilities in these areas. A combination of education and practical training can prepare an individual for a career in forensic science.

Most of the Nation's practicing forensic scientists are employed in ***crime laboratories*** associated with law enforcement or other government agencies. Forensic scientists come to the profession with diverse undergraduate science degrees. They also may go on to earn graduate degrees. This document contains suggestions for model programs in forensic science at both the undergraduate and graduate levels. A combination of personal, professional, and academic criteria will influence a prospective forensic science examiner's suitability for employment.

Government entities' hiring processes are driven by civil service regulations or collective bargaining agreements that are specific to the branch of government, State, or locality. Private laboratories have their own hiring processes. The hiring process may include written and practical tests, phone interviews, and one-on-one personal interviews or interviews conducted by a panel. New employees may be hired provisionally or go through a probationary period. ***Provisional employment*** offers may be revoked either before or after reporting for duty.

Model Candidate

A model candidate for all forensic science practices possesses personal integrity, holds a baccalaureate degree (at a minimum) in the natural sciences, and has additional KSAs that fulfill the recommendations set forth in this *Guide*.

Personal characteristics

Because forensic science is part of the criminal justice system, personal honesty, integrity, and scientific objectivity are paramount. Those seeking careers in this field should be aware that background checks similar to those required for law enforcement officers are likely to be a condition of employment. The following may be conducted and/or reviewed before an employment offer is made and may remain as ongoing conditions of employment (this list is not all inclusive):

- Drug tests.
- History of drug use.
- Criminal history.

- ***Personal associations.***
- Polygraph examination.
- Driving record.
- Past work performance.
- Credit history.
- Medical or physical examination.

Personal candor in these areas is critical. In addition, an individual's history of community service and outside activities may also be considered.

Academic qualifications

Forensic scientists need to have a strong fundamental background in the natural sciences. For example, new hires who analyze drugs, DNA, trace, and toxicological evidence in forensic science laboratories typically have a degree in chemistry, biochemistry, biology, or forensic science from an accredited institution. Although forensic scientists involved in the recognition and comparison of patterns (such as latent prints, firearms, and questioned documents) historically may not have been required to have a degree, the trend in the field is to strengthen the academic requirements for these disciplines and require a baccalaureate degree, preferably in a science. The academic qualifications required for some of the emerging disciplines, such as digital evidence, are currently being defined and will be published by the appropriate groups. Achieving the appropriate academic qualifications is discussed in greater detail later in this *Guide*.

Copies of diplomas and formal academic transcripts are generally required as proof of academic qualification. Awards, publications, internships, and student activities may be used to differentiate applicants. Claims in this regard are subject to verification through the background investigation process.

Professional skills

A variety of skills are essential to an individual's effectiveness as a forensic science professional, including:

- Critical thinking (quantitative reasoning and problem solving).
- Decisionmaking.
- Good laboratory practices.
- Awareness of laboratory safety.
- Observation and attention to detail.
- Computer proficiency.
- Interpersonal skills.
- Public speaking.
- Oral and written communication.
- Time management.
- Prioritization of tasks.

For some of these skills, systematic tools are available that may be used to measure skill or proficiency at or after the time of hire.

Model Career Path for Forensic Scientists

A model career path for a forensic scientist begins with formal education and continues with training, postgraduate education, certification, and professional membership. Exhibit 1 depicts stages of a career path in forensic science.

Exhibit 1. **A Model Career Path in Forensic Science**

Credentials

A forensic scientist's career path should demonstrate continued professional development that is documented by credentials. A credential is a formal recognition of a professional's knowledge, skills, and abilities. Indicators of professional standing include academic credentials, professional credentials, training credentials, and competency tests. Exhibit 1 underscores for students, laboratory managers, agency personnel, and the public how ***credentialing*** can positively impact the overall effectiveness of forensic science practice.

Implementation: Keys to a Career in Forensic Science

Pre-employment preparation

Competitive candidates can demonstrate the knowledge, skills, and abilities that establish their readiness for a forensic science position. These KSAs may include areas important to all potential forensic science practitioners, including but not limited to quality assurance, ethics, professional standards of behavior, evidence control, report writing, scientific method, inductive and deductive reasoning, statistics, and safety. Documentation of coursework and practical experiences involving these KSAs can significantly enhance the objective information available to an agency evaluating potential new hires.

On-the-job training

After hire, on-the-job training by the hiring agency is common. This initial training is generally completed within 6 months to 3 years of the date of hire, depending on the trainee, agency, and forensic science specialty. Some specialties have established peer-based objective standards adopted throughout the field, while others vary from agency to agency.

Certification

Accreditation applies to forensic science *laboratories*, whereas certification applies to *analysts* or *examiners*. Individuals whose competencies have been certified by an independent, peer-based, appropriately credentialed certifying body are highly desirable to employers.

Outstanding laboratories seek certification from an organization that is accredited by the Forensic Specialties Accreditation Board or another program that is based on nationally or internationally recognized standards (see appendix C). A credible certification program requires a meaningful evaluation of credentials, examination, an ethics component, and periodic recertification. Recertification requires a person to undergo a minimum amount of continuing education and may require demonstration of continued competency. Certification has been used by some employers as a prerequisite for employment and/or advancement, and it may enhance an individual's credibility as an expert witness.

Professional involvement

While casework is the primary focus of a forensic scientist, he or she can also strive to advance the profession. This may be accomplished through professional involvement: research; mentoring; teaching; and participating in professional organizations, community outreach, publishing, and other professional activities.

Summary

A strong educational background in the natural sciences, personal attributes such as honesty and integrity, and additional professional skills are necessary to prepare a candidate for a career in forensic science. In addition to formal academic education and employer-provided training, a level of self-motivated professional development, including certification and involvement in the field, provides tremendous growth opportunities for both experienced professionals and those entering the field.

Undergraduate Curriculum in Forensic Science

Introduction

Forensic science is an applied science that covers an array of disciplines. Regardless of the area of forensic science pursued, an undergraduate degree in forensic science should be interdisciplinary, combining a strong foundation in the natural sciences with extensive laboratory experience.

A model undergraduate forensic science degree program should provide a strong and credible science foundation that emphasizes the scientific method and the application of problem-solving skills in both classroom and laboratory settings. Graduates of an undergraduate forensic science program should have acquired KSAs that include scientific writing, public speaking, laboratory skills and safety practices, and computer software application skills.

The strengths of a model undergraduate forensic science degree include—

- Preparation for becoming a forensic science professional.
- Opportunities to establish a network of forensic science contacts.
- An educational background directly linked to the work in a forensic science laboratory.
- Exposure to the breadth of forensic science disciplines.
- Acculturation into the forensic science and justice communities.
- Provision of a foundation for professional certification.
- Emphasis on a wide range of courses (e.g., public speaking, ethics, and statistics) that may not be required in the curriculums of other natural science majors.

Most forensic science employment occurs in a laboratory setting. Results of laboratory analyses are typically used by law enforcement to investigate crimes, identify or eliminate suspects, and assist courts in reaching fair and just determinations. Although not exhaustive, the following list presents types of evidence typically examined by professionals working in forensic science laboratories (also see "What Is 'Criminalistics'?"):

- Controlled substances (drugs).
- Toxicological specimens, including body tissues, body fluids, and breath.
- Trace evidence, including hairs, fibers, paint, glass, and explosives and fire debris.
- Biological specimens, including DNA.
- Firearms.
- Fingerprints.
- Impression evidence, including toolmarks, tiremarks, and shoeprints.

- Questioned documents.
- Crime scene.

The science curriculum described herein is not generally required for prospective crime scene specialists; however, it is highly recommended. Students seeking to work in alternative areas of forensic science, such as forensic computer sciences, may require other curriculums or further specialized training (see appendix A).

Model Curriculum: Undergraduate Degree in Forensic Science

This section of the *Guide* provides minimum recommendations for a model undergraduate degree in forensic science. Such a degree provides an educational foundation that meets the current hiring requirements of forensic science laboratories. This curriculum emphasizes the strong natural science foundation that is essential to prepare a student for a successful career in forensic science. Refer to exhibit 2 for an overview of the model curriculum.

This curriculum is not designed to produce case-ready forensic scientists. Laboratory managers, educators, and students may realize that prior to beginning casework, additional on-the-job training and possible postgraduate studies may be necessary to meet the specific needs of the individual employer.

Peer-based working groups have promulgated specific education requirements (see appendixes D and E). Forensic science laboratories and graduate programs may require more than the recommended credit hours of specific coursework.

University general education

General education courses are courses that the university requires the student to take. They may include language, humanities, social sciences, mathematics, technical writing, computer science, and public speaking. The actual number of credit hours required may vary from university to university but generally ranges from 36 to 40. Some forensic degree coursework may count toward fulfilling this requirement. Carefully selected general education courses can complement the student's main program of study.

Natural science core

Certain natural science courses are required for any student in forensic science. Unlike other criminal justice professionals, a forensic scientist requires a foundation in chemistry, biology, physics, and mathematics.

The minimum general core requirements recommended for undergraduate forensic science programs (34–38 total credit hours) include—

- General chemistry I and II and lab for science majors (8 credit hours).
- Organic chemistry I and II and lab (8 credit hours).
- Biology I and II for science majors (4–8 credit hours). (Classes with laboratory components are preferable, if available.)
- Physics I and II for science majors and lab (8 credit hours).
- Calculus (3 credit hours).
- Statistics for science majors (3 credit hours).

Exhibit 2. **Sample Curriculum for Forensic Science Undergraduate Degrees**[a]

	Biology	Chemistry/Trace Evidence/Controlled Substances	Toxicology	Firearms/Impression Evidence/Questioned Documents/Prints
University General Education (36–40 hrs)	Courses required by the university, which may include language, humanities, social sciences, technical writing, mathematics, computer science, and public speaking. Credit hours required will vary from university to university. Some forensic degree coursework may count toward fulfilling these requirements.			
Natural Science Core (34–38 hrs)	Biology I, II[b] Calculus General Chemistry I, II[b] Organic Chemistry I, II[b] Physics I, II[b] Statistics	Biology I Calculus General Chemistry I, II Organic Chemistry I, II Physics I, II Statistics	Biology I Calculus General Chemistry I, II Organic Chemistry I, II Physics I, II Statistics	Biology I Calculus General Chemistry I, II Organic Chemistry I, II Physics I, II Statistics
Specialized Core (12 hrs)	Biochemistry Genetics Instrumental Analysis Molecular Biology	Analytic Chemistry Quantitative[b] Inorganic Chemistry Instrumental Analysis Physical Chemistry	Analytic Chemistry Quantitative Biochemistry Instrumental Analysis Physical Chemistry	Inorganic Chemistry Instrumental Analysis Optics/Lasers Physical Chemistry
Forensic Science Core (6 hrs)	Forensic Science Survey Forensic Professional Practice[c]	Forensic Science Survey Forensic Professional Practice	Forensic Science Survey Forensic Professional Practice	Forensic Science Survey Forensic Professional Practice
Forensic Laboratory Science (9 hrs)	Forensic Biology ***Internship*** Microscopy Physical Methods	Forensic Chemistry Internship Microscopy Physical Methods	Forensic Chemistry Internship Microscopy Physical Methods	Internship Microscopy Physical Methods
Additional Courses[d] (19 hrs)	Cell Biology Introduction to Criminal Justice Legal Evidence Microbiology Population Genetics Immunology Public Speaking	Advanced Instrumental Analysis Drugs Introduction to Criminal Justice Legal Evidence Analytical Toxicology Materials Science Pharmacology Public Speaking	Advanced Instrumental Analysis Drugs Introduction to Criminal Justice Legal Evidence Analytical Toxicology Pharmacology Public Speaking	Crime Scene Image Analysis Introduction to Criminal Justice Legal Evidence Materials Science

a. These examples are based on a minimum of 120 semester hours to obtain a degree. Credit hours as described above are meant to indicate semester credit hours.
b. Laboratory courses.
c. This course includes ethics, testimony, evidence, chain of custody, etc.
d. Electives listed here are not exhaustive, and students may wish to tailor courses according to their areas of concentration.

Specialized science courses

An undergraduate degree in forensic science is expected to be an interdisciplinary degree that includes substantial laboratory work and an emphasis on advanced (i.e., upper level) coursework in chemistry or biology. Students can use these additional courses to begin to specialize along a forensic science discipline track, such as forensic biology or forensic chemistry.

Specialized science courses may be selected from any of the following (minimum 12 credit hours and minimum of 2 laboratory courses):

- Biochemistry.
- Molecular biology.
- Genetics.
- Population genetics.

- Inorganic chemistry.
- Analytical/quantitative chemistry.
- Physical chemistry.
- Instrumental analysis.
- Cell biology.
- Pharmacology.
- Calculus II.
- Microbiology.

If pursuing a career as a forensic DNA examiner, coursework in the above areas is required by the *FBI Quality Assurance Standards for Forensic DNA Testing Laboratories.*[1]

Forensic science core

It is essential to cover certain forensic science topics in specific courses or as portions of courses that combine several topics. Include the following topics as ***core elements*** in the forensic science curriculum:

- Introduction to law/justice system.
- Ethics/professional practice.
- Forensic science specialty overview (survey course).

Summary of Credit Hours

- 36–40 hours of general university requirements.
- 46–50 hours of natural and specified science courses.
- 15 hours of forensic science courses (9 of which should include laboratory work).
- 19 hours of additional courses.

Total: 120 credit hours

- Evidence identification, collection, and processing.
- Quality assurance.
- Courtroom testimony.
- Technical or scientific writing.

Forensic science laboratory courses

In addition to a strong foundation in the natural sciences, forensic science professionals are expected to recognize concepts integral to forensic science, such as individualization, reconstruction, association, and chain of custody of evidence. Because the work product of a forensic scientist is used by the justice system, it is expected to meet legal as well as scientific standards. The following courses are designed to give the student an understanding of the application of scientific analysis to the legal system (a minimum of 15 credit hours, for which a minimum of 9 credit hours are expected to be laboratory science courses):

- Forensic chemistry and lab (3).
- Forensic biology and lab (3).
- Physical methods in forensic science and lab (3).
- Internship (up to 6) or independent study/research (up to 6).
- Microscopy and lab (3).

Additional courses

Students are advised to select additional courses (approximately 19 credit hours) that give them greater depth in their specific area of concentration (see exhibit 2 for examples). Additional courses may be necessary to satisfy admission requirements into some graduate programs.

Implementation: Keys to Ensuring Curriculum Success

Significant additional funding is necessary to bolster existing forensic science undergraduate programs and to create new programs. Funding can create an incentive for programs to provide students with the highest quality forensic science education. The following are essential for the proper implementation of a successful undergraduate academic program:

Objectives and assessments of institutional effectiveness

A program is expected to provide documented, measurable objectives, including expected outcomes for graduates. The program is expected to regularly assess its progress against its objectives and use the results to identify areas for program improvement and to modify the program objectives.

Institutional support

A forensic science curriculum is expected to enjoy a level of institutional support equal to other natural science programs (e.g., biology or chemistry). Forensic science undergraduate programs that are undersupported can be upgraded according to these recommendations, and new programs can be eliminated if the proper facilities and operating budgets are not available. Funding sources could include competitive Federal funding, other public and private sources, and the host college or university. Institutions are expected to provide an appropriate variety of courses and offer them often enough to allow students to complete the program in a reasonable amount of time.

Full-time faculty

An adequate number of full-time faculty members ensures continuity and stability to cover the curriculum and to allow an appropriate mix of instruction and scholarly activity. The faculty members' interests and qualifications are expected to be sufficient to teach the courses and plan and modify the courses and curriculum. Faculty members are expected to have knowledge and experience appropriate to the course being taught and to recognize advisory duties as a valued part of their workload.

Adjunct faculty

Practicing forensic scientists, often required as adjunct faculty, are expected to have the knowledge and experience appropriate to the course being taught. However, it is essential that full-time faculty oversee the curriculum for all coursework and maintain institutional standards.

Facilities

Laboratories and computing facilities that are available, accessible, and adequately equipped and supported are essential to enable students to complete their coursework and support the teaching needs and scholarly activities of the faculty. Such institutional facilities as the library, classrooms, and offices are expected to be adequate to support the program objectives. A library where faculty and students have access to books, periodicals, and electronic resources (with adequate support for database searching) is essential to a successful program. The institution is also expected to subscribe to several referred forensic science journals.

Student support

It is essential that each student has adequate and reasonable access to equipment currently being used in forensic science laboratories and appropriate to the course of instruction. This equipment may be located in the forensic science department, natural science department, or nearby cooperating operational forensic science laboratories. Students should be afforded ample opportunity to interact with their instructors and be offered timely and informed guidance about program requirements, course options, and career opportunities.

Faculty support

Sufficient support for faculty enables the program to attract and retain high-quality faculty capable of supporting the program's objectives. Support is expected to include opportunities to attend professional meetings, recognition of scholarly activities, adequate time for administrative duties, and clerical support.

Collaboration with forensic science laboratories

Academic forensic science programs are expected to establish working relationships with forensic science laboratories, if possible. Collaboration can provide meaningful internships, employment opportunities, guest lecturers, adjunct faculty, direct interaction with forensic scientists, and cooperative research.

Accreditation

The institution granting the degree is expected to be accredited by an accrediting body recognized by the U.S. Department of Education.

At the time of this writing, there is no mechanism for accrediting forensic science undergraduate programs. When this mechanism is implemented, it is strongly recommended that all such programs seek accreditation.[2] Accreditation provides many benefits, including—

- An external means of program validation.
- A tool to help students select a program.
- A means for forensic scientists and potential employers to judge graduates' credentials.
- An improvement of program quality.
- A high level of competency for graduates.

Summary

Forensic science is an applied multidisciplinary profession based on the natural sciences. Therefore, it is essential that students studying forensic science have education and training consistent with this scientific foundation. The strengths of an undergraduate forensic science education include professional preparation, networking, links to laboratories, work-related knowledge, and preparation for professional certification. Recommendations regarding this scientific foundation have been set forth as best practices for a proposed forensic science undergraduate curriculum. These recommendations include core natural science courses, extensive laboratory experience in both the natural and forensic sciences, special topics in forensic science, and other supporting coursework. The forensic science undergraduate degree is designed to prepare students for entry into traditional forensic science laboratory employment and for graduate-level education and training in many other disciplines.

In addition, this section provides recommendations for implementing a successful forensic science program, including program objectives and assessments, institutional support, faculty qualifications, the role of adjunct faculty, facility requirements, support of students and faculty, collaborations with forensic science laboratories, and program accreditation.

Notes

1. Federal Bureau of Investigation, *Quality Assurance Standards for Forensic DNA Testing Laboratories,* Washington, DC: U.S. Department of Justice, Federal Bureau of Investigation, 1998, http://www.fbi.gov/congress/congress02/forensicstd.htm.

2. In fall 2003, the Forensic Science Education Programs Accreditation Commission (FEPAC)—a committee of the American Academy of Forensic Sciences—began a pilot accreditation program. FEPAC's standards are based on this *Guide*. FEPAC plans to begin formal accreditation of undergraduate and graduate forensic science programs in 2004.

Graduate Curriculum in Forensic Science

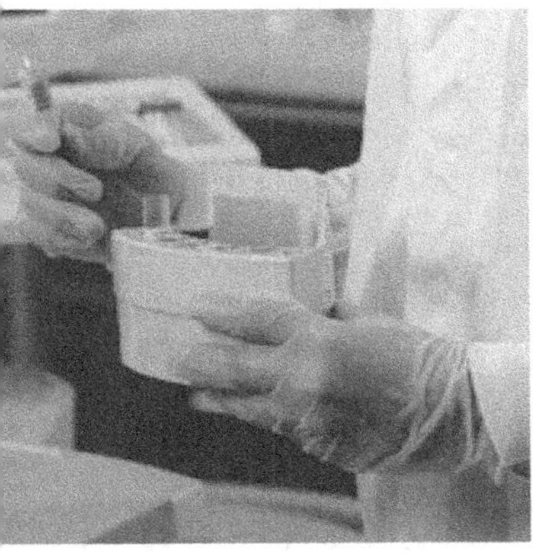

Introduction

The minimum prerequisite for entry into a graduate-level forensic science program is a baccalaureate degree in forensic science or a natural science, in addition to such college or university requirements as grade point average and Graduate Record Examination scores.

A fundamental background in the natural sciences is central to the education of a forensic scientist who examines physical evidence in a laboratory setting. A graduate-level forensic science program is expected to do more than educate students in theoretical concepts. It should provide the student with critical thinking ability, problem-solving skills, and advanced, discipline-specific knowledge. It is likely that increasing numbers of forensic scientists may seek graduate-level education in the forensic or natural sciences, which may facilitate career advancement.

Most graduate programs in forensic science can lead to a master of science (M.S.) degree. The graduate curriculum recommendations later in this chapter refer to programs that award an M.S. in forensic science. Students earning this degree are expected to be prepared for employment in operational forensic science laboratories.

A need also exists for doctoral programs in the natural sciences with an emphasis on forensic science research. Advanced education is necessary to prepare forensic scientists, academicians, and researchers for leadership roles in public and private laboratories and academic institutions. A full discussion of forensic science doctoral programs goes beyond the scope of this *Guide*.

The forensic sciences encompass many disciplines. This section focuses on the following:

- Controlled substances (drugs).
- Toxicological specimens, including body tissues, body fluids, and breath.
- Trace evidence, including hairs, fibers, paint, glass, and explosives and fire debris.
- Biological specimens, including DNA.
- Firearms.
- Fingerprints.
- Impression evidence, including toolmarks, tiremarks, and shoeprints.
- Questioned documents.
- Crime scene.

An institution's educational objectives and resources govern the nature of any graduate program, and these can vary considerably. The institution is expected to be strongly committed to programs intended to prepare students for a career in forensic science in accordance with these best practices.

Model Curriculum: Graduate Degree in Forensic Science

Existing graduate programs in North America include master of science in forensic science/criminalistics and master of science in a natural science (e.g., chemistry, biology) with a track or emphasis in forensic science. Program and other considerations have led to a wide variation in the content and structure of these programs.

An exemplary program will contain the following elements (discussed in detail below):

- Forensic science topics.
- Rigorous academic coursework in a specialized area(s).
- Research component.
- Laboratory component.
- Interaction with operational forensic science laboratories and professional societies.
- Qualified faculty with appropriate forensic science experience.
- Sufficient faculty-to-student ratio and support personnel.
- Adequate academic resources (library, journal subscriptions, laboratory space, equipment, etc.).
- Student support in the form of assistantships and/or fellowships.

Curriculum recommendations

A bachelor of science degree in a forensic or natural science (or its equivalent coursework in a relevant field) is preferred for entering a forensic science graduate program. At a minimum, the courses described in exhibit 2 are expected to be prerequisites for entry into a graduate forensic science program. Other degrees may provide sufficient prerequisite courses for consideration.

Master's programs in forensic science can be organized in many ways to reflect the institution's mission, the available facilities, and the interests and capabilities of the students and faculty. Regardless of how the program is organized, all graduate students are required to take the core curriculum consisting of a minimum of 30 semester credit hours. Students who enter a graduate forensic science program with undergraduate coursework or degrees that emphasized forensic science may have their specific coursework adjusted to reflect this background.

Syllabuses are expected to be current and describe the content of the course and required textbook(s).

An exemplary graduate forensic science curriculum will contain the following topics:

- Crime scenes.
- Physical evidence concepts.
- Law/science interface.
- Ethics and professional responsibility.
- Quality assurance.
- Specific course(s) covering the following topic areas:
  - —Analytical chemistry and instrumental methods of analysis.
  - —Drug chemistry/toxicology.
  - —Microscopy and ***materials analysis.***
  - —Forensic biology.
  - —Pattern evidence.

Forensic science programs may offer specializations, tracks, or concentrations in different areas such as analytical chemistry or molecular genetics. All forensic science programs are expected to offer rigorous graduate-level academic coursework in appropriate subjects. The syllabus descriptions should indicate that the courses are advanced, comprehensive, and current. Advanced courses may be scheduled regularly to enable students to take the courses in proper sequence and with reasonable flexibility. In addition, it is expected that a number of specialized graduate-level courses may be required to suit the students' interests and enhance the research experience. A graduate seminar is recommended that includes regular attendance at presentations by experts on original research and other relevant topics.

Research component

The student is expected to conduct a research project, prepare a written report, and present the results of the research in a public forum prior to graduation. The research component of the program may include preparatory coursework in research methods and statistics. The ideal research project is well defined, stands a reasonable chance of completion in the time available, and requires the student to use advanced concepts and a variety of experimental techniques and instruments. Research in forensic science advances the body of knowledge and elevates the status of the profession.

Communication skills

Effective written and oral communication skills are essential to the well-trained scientist. Forensic scientists are expected to be proficient in written and oral communication. Frequent exercises in writing and oral presentation are expected to be part of the forensic science curriculum and be critically evaluated by the forensic science faculty.

Institutional accreditation

The institution granting the degree is expected to be accredited by an accrediting body that is recognized by the U.S. Department of Education.

Faculty requirements

At least 75 percent of full-time science faculty teaching in a forensic science graduate program should have an appropriate doctoral degree; faculty who have had experience working in a forensic science laboratory are preferred. The scientific and educational capabilities of the faculty should be distributed over the major program areas, and courses should be taught by persons qualified in each specialty. Also, an adequate number of highly competent faculty allows for regular offerings of the full range of courses needed for graduate education in forensic science.

Library requirements and information retrieval

A library where faculty and students have access to books, periodicals, and electronic resources (with adequate support for database searching) is essential to a successful program. An institution with a broad spectrum of research activity may require extensive holdings and is expected to subscribe to several referred forensic science journals. Further, students are also expected to learn how to retrieve specific information from the enormous and rapidly expanding literature.

Classroom and laboratory requirements

Classrooms and laboratories are expected to meet appropriate academic and safety requirements for the number of students in the program. In addition to instructional laboratories, faculty and students are expected to have access to laboratories with research-appropriate facilities, equipment, and instrumentation.

Laboratory experience

The laboratory component is expected to include the use of appropriate instrumentation and give students sufficient hands-on knowledge of forensic science and competence to—

- Anticipate, recognize, and respond properly to chemical and biological hazards.
- Keep legible and complete laboratory records.
- Conduct qualitative and quantitative analyses.
- Use and understand instrumentation and fundamental techniques.
- Analyze data and evaluate experimental results.
- Assess reliability of results and draw reasonable conclusions.
- Communicate effectively through oral and written reports.

Interaction with operational laboratories

Academic programs are expected to interact with operational forensic science laboratories. Cooperative efforts may take the form of internships, adjunct faculty interaction, staying current in the discipline, collaborative research, visiting scientist programs, and seminars.

An option within a graduate program may be a residency or fellowship based on the model that medical schools use that combines formal, structured specialty training with an academic program. These programs can serve as a valuable component of a comprehensive and experiential training program. Such a program can provide hands-on training and experience in a forensic specialty so the student can be ready to perform the casework after completing the program. This program option may include discipline-specific simulated casework analysis, oral boards, moot courts, data review and interpretation, and report writing. This option can extend the normal time for completion of a graduate degree.

Implementation: Keys to Ensuring Graduate Program Success

Funding

Increased funding is essential for graduate forensic science education to meet the demonstrated needs of the profession. Currently, no sustainable source of State or Federal funding exists to support graduate education or research in forensic science. The National Institute of Justice has traditionally provided virtually all research funding for the forensic sciences, but additional funding from alternative sources is essential.

In addition to State and private sources, funding may be available from the following Federal agencies: U.S. Department of Justice, National Science Foundation, National Institutes of Health, U.S. Department of Energy, National Security Agency, U.S. Department of Education, and U.S. Department of Commerce. In light of homeland security and terrorism concerns, funding may also be sought from the Centers for Disease Control and Prevention, Federal Aviation Administration, U.S. Department of Defense, Food and Drug Administration, Federal Emergency

Management Agency, and U.S. Department of Homeland Security.

Support for graduate student education is essential to successful future operations of the graduate programs in forensic science. Ideally, this support may be provided to educational institutions in the form of competitive training grants. In addition, individual graduate research fellowships may be available. Programs may also take advantage of existing institutional graduate support mechanisms.

Appropriate legislative bodies can allow programs to forgive student loans for graduates who obtain full-time employment in public forensic science institutions.

In addition to research and student support, funding also is needed for the acquisition and maintenance of equipment and major research instrumentation and laboratory renovation. Institutions offering forensic science programs need to provide for ongoing costs associated with the laboratory component of the curriculum and program administration.

Accreditation

At the time of this writing, no mechanism exists for accrediting forensic science graduate programs. When this mechanism is implemented, it is strongly recommended that all programs seek accreditation. Accreditation provides many benefits, including—

- An external means of program validation.
- A valuable tool to help students select a program.
- A means for forensic scientists and potential employers to judge the credentials of graduates.
- Improvement of program quality.
- A high level of competency for graduates.

Training and Continuing Education in Forensic Science

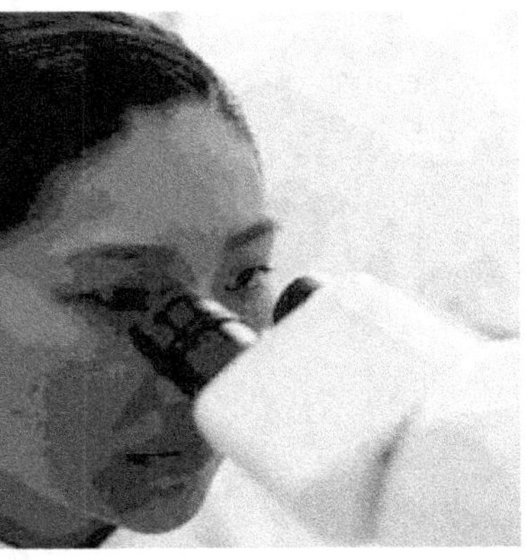

Introduction

This section outlines model criteria and implementation approaches for the training and ***continuing professional development*** of forensic scientists. Model criteria are presented separately for training to attain competency and for post-competency continuing professional development.

Training is the formal, structured process through which a forensic scientist reaches a level of scientific knowledge and expertise required to conduct specific forensic analyses. Appropriate training is required before an individual is assigned case analysis responsibilities.

Continuing professional development is the mechanism through which a forensic scientist remains current or advances to a higher level of expertise, specialization, or responsibility. All forensic scientists have an ongoing obligation to remain current in their field through continuing education and other developmental activities noted in exhibit 1. Similarly, laboratory management and its parent agency have an ongoing responsibility to provide support and opportunities for this continuing professional development.

Recognition of any training or continuing professional development requires proper documentation. The agency or training entity is expected to keep a permanent, official training record and provide the trainee with a copy. The trainee is encouraged to keep a personal copy of the training record. The training record may include—

- Documentation that entry requirements have been satisfied.
- Detailed description of program structure, content, and assessment.
- Trainee performance documentation.
- Certificate or statement of successful completion of the training program.

Model Criteria

Model criteria are intended as a guide for formulating training and continuing professional development programs. These model criteria can provide a common framework across forensic disciplines and thereby help ensure that programs are consistent and contain essential elements.

Training

Model training criteria include entry requirements, program structure and content, assessment mechanisms, and documentation.

Entry requirements should include—

- Specified minimum academic and experiential requirements consistent with recognized, peer-defined standards (e.g., scientific working groups, American Society of Crime Laboratory Directors/ Laboratory Accreditation Board, and

American Board of Criminalists) (see appendixes C, D, and E).

- Applicant awareness that ongoing background security clearances and random drug testing may be required. Factors such as drug use, credit and criminal history, and personal references may affect career opportunities.

Exemplary program structure includes the following written components:

- Learning objectives.
- Instructor qualifications.
- Student requirements.
- Detailed syllabus.
- Performance goals.
- Periodic assessments.
- ***Competency testing.***

Program content can be designed to include both discipline-specific and core elements. Core elements are essential topics that lay the foundation for entry into professional practice regardless of the specialty area. They include the following:

- Standards of conduct—includes professional ethics training.
- Safety—includes biological, chemical, and physical hazards.
- Policy—includes such administrative and laboratory policies as standard operating procedures, quality assurance, accreditation, and security.
- Legal—includes expert testimony, depositions, rules of evidence, criminal and civil law and procedures, and evidence authentication.
- Evidence handling—includes interdisciplinary issues; recognition, collection, and preservation of evidence; and chain of custody.
- Communication—includes written, verbal, and nonverbal communication skills; report writing; exhibit and pretrial preparation; and trial presentation.

Discipline-specific elements guided by recognized peer-defined standards can be incorporated as appropriate. Topics include—

- History of the discipline.
- Relevant literature.
- Methodologies and validation studies.
- Instrumentation.
- Statistics.
- Knowledge of related fields.
- Testimony.

The trainee's progress is expected to be assessed at appropriate intervals. Assessment mechanisms may include—

- Oral exams.
- Written exams.
- ***Laboratory practicals*** and ***laboratory exercises.***
- Mock trials.
- Assessment of technical performance by appropriate senior staff.

Continuing professional development

Continuing professional development encompasses competency maintenance, skill enhancement, and other aspects of professional activities. It is important that continuing professional development be structured, measurable, and documented.

Structure. Courses for continuing professional development are expected to include the following predefined components:

- Learning objectives.
- Instructor qualifications.
- Detailed syllabus or program description.
- Assessment.
- Documentation.

Measurement. Assessment mechanisms include—

- Oral exams or reports.
- Written exams or reports.
- Peer-reviewed publications.
- Instructor or presenter evaluation.
- Laboratory practicals and exercises.
- Observation of technical performance.

Documentation. An agency is expected to keep a permanent, official record of employees' continuing professional development activities. The employee is encouraged to keep a personal copy of his/her record. The agency's record is expected to include a description of the activity, its format, and documentation of performance (when available), such as academic credit, continuing education credit, certificates, and/or abstracts of proceedings.

Implementation: Making the Most of Training and Continuing Professional Development

Training and continuing professional development based on the model criteria can be implemented in a variety of ways to maximize opportunities, minimize costs, and ensure high standards of professional practice. The examples below offer guidance for implementation.

Approaches

Different disciplines require varying levels and combinations of approaches. The approach depends on the relative degree of academic and experiential learning required to attain and maintain competency. For example, the questioned-document discipline may require more experience-based skill, whereas forensic biology may require more academic knowledge.

Some peer groups (see for example, appendixes C and D) provide guidance regarding frequency of training and continuing professional development. It is recommended that this guidance be considered when choosing any approach. Some approaches include—

- Instructor led.
- Professional conferences/seminars.
- ***Distributed learning.***
- ***Apprenticeship.***
- ***Residency.***
- Internship.
- Teaching and presentations by trainee/employee.
- Independent learning.

Administration

It is recommended that forensic laboratories establish a process to oversee, coordinate, and document all training and continuing professional development. Training and continuing professional development programs are expected to undergo external periodic audits.

It is recommended that continuing education and training courses include—

- Qualified instructor(s).
- Written course syllabus/outline.
- Written course objectives.
- Instructor/course evaluation.
- Mechanism for student assessment.
- Documentation of student performance.
- Quantifiable element, such as continuing education units, academic credits, number of hours, or points.

Although seminars, lectures, professional meetings, and inservice classes may be less structured than a formal course, they also add to the professional development of forensic scientists. Content and attendance are expected to be documented and available for external audits.

Sources

The sources of training and continuing professional development can be internal and/or external to a forensic science laboratory. Training partnerships are valuable because they provide broad perspectives and facilitate consistency of professional practice. Sources include—

- Government agencies.
- Academic institutions.
- Training academies and institutions.
- Private industries and organizations.
- Professional societies.
- Mentors.

Funding

Resources are needed to properly support training and continuing professional development. In addition to their regular duties, qualified forensic scientists and supervisors are expected to receive time to continue professional development and to mentor trainees. Agency management is expected to plan for any effects that reallocating laboratory resources may have on case productivity.

Agencies can partner to develop and provide intensive formal discipline-specific programs for trainees. These programs can relieve operational forensic science laboratories of the in-house mentoring needed to qualify individuals to conduct casework. This partnering model also can be extended to continuing professional development, with agencies working together to develop and provide standardized training curriculums and materials for use across several agencies. Although these partnerships can significantly reduce costs, funding for student attendance may still be needed.

When considering the costs of continuing professional development, some scientific working groups recommend minimum mandatory "contact hours." For example, the Scientific Working Group for the Analysis of Forensic Drug Samples (SWGDRUG) recommends that a minimum of 20 contact hours per year be devoted to continuing professional development for each drug examiner. *FBI Quality Assurance Standards for Forensic DNA Testing Laboratories* require 1 day of continuing professional development per year, and this has been adopted as the requirement for DNA examiners for compliance with ASCLD/LAB standards.

In the absence of external guidelines on contact time per year, some agencies impose their own contact time requirements. Alternatively, some agencies

specify a training and continuing professional development budget of, for example, $1,000–$1,500 per year for each examiner. Such funds are used to support travel and fees for both outside learning opportunities and implementation of in-house programs. It is recommended that 1–3 percent of the total forensic science laboratory budget be allocated for training and continuing professional development.

The professionalism expected of forensic science staff requires that appropriate resources for training and development be provided by the parent agency. Forensic science is a labor-intensive undertaking, in which the quality, experience, and technical currency of personnel performing the work are paramount. Neglecting ongoing staff training and professional development can lead to organizational failure to meet stakeholder agencies' service goals and quality requirements.

Regardless of the mechanism used, it is essential that a reasonable foundation be put in place to offset the direct and indirect costs of an adequate program of training and continuing professional development.

Summary

Model criteria are presented as a framework for achieving and maintaining professional competency in forensic sciences. Implementation of these criteria will extend learning opportunities and promote high standards of professional practice.

Glossary

Apprenticeship: A relationship where an individual works for an entity while learning skills.

Biology: The science concerned with the growth, development, and functioning of living things.

Certification: A peer-based voluntary process of credentialing that involves objective review of academic degrees, minimum mandatory experience in the discipline, and successful completion of a written examination. Certifying organizations should satisfy the requirements of ISO Guide 17024 for the accreditation of certifying bodies. See appendix C for a list of certifying organizations.

Chemistry: The science that studies the structures, functions, transformations, and interactions of basic elements and matter.

Competency Testing: The evaluation of a person's ability to perform work in a functional area prior to the performance of independent casework.

Continuing Professional Development: The mechanism through which an individual remains current or advances to a higher level of expertise, specialization, or responsibility.

Core Elements: Concepts, theories, and information that represent the foundation of a science or area of study.

Credentialing: Formal recognition of a professional's knowledge, skills, and abilities (KSAs) in a particular field of expertise. This recognition is documented by academic degrees, professional certifications, and completion of specialty training programs.

Crime Laboratories: Facilities that receive, process, and analyze evidence (obtained through civil or criminal investigations) using scientific or technical methods and opinion testimony with respect to such physical evidence in a court of law; equivalent to forensic science laboratories.

Criminalistics: The profession and scientific discipline of recognizing, identifying, individualizing, and evaluating physical evidence in legal proceedings by the application of the natural sciences.

Distributed Learning: Educational methods that use models of distant, distributed, or remote education, such as video, the Internet, networked multimedia, and independent or proctored study models.

Forensic Science: The profession of assisting criminal and civil investigations and litigation through science.

Forensic Science Laboratories: Facilities that receive, process, and analyze evidence obtained through civil or criminal investigations using scientific or technical methods and opinion testimony with respect to such physical evidence in a court of law; equivalent to crime laboratories.

Internship: An indepth educational or training program that offers a period of supervised practical experience in a forensic science setting.

Knowledge, Skills, and Abilities (KSAs): The level of information, qualifications, and experience needed to perform assigned tasks. Knowledge refers to acquired principles and practices related to a particular job; skills refer to acquired psychomotor behaviors; and abilities are the talents, observable behaviors, or acquired dexterity.

Laboratory Exercises: An educational activity where scientific concepts, principles, and methods that relate to laboratory procedures are demonstrated.

Laboratory Practicals: An educational testing situation that emphasizes hands-on methods and procedures.

Materials Analysis: The characterization of composition and structure (including defects) of a material that is significant for a particular product, study of properties, or use. In forensic science, this typically refers but is not limited to the analysis of trace evidence.

Natural Sciences: Sciences, such as biology, chemistry, or physics, that deal with the objects, phenomena, or laws of nature and the physical world.

Personal Associations: Social and professional relationships that may reflect on the morals, values, and citizenship of an individual.

Pre-Employment Qualifications: The suggested milestones, including a required degree, personal character qualifications, and professional skills, that should be obtained before seeking employment in a crime laboratory or a forensic science laboratory.

Provisional Employment: Introductory period of employment that allows the employee and agency to determine if the employee is suited for the job. During the provisional employment period, employees may be terminated at the discretion of the appointing authority, without access to a grievance procedure. A normal provisional employment period is 6 to 12 months; however, it can be extended as specified in the agency's policies.

Professional Involvement: Activities that advance a profession, such as research, mentoring, teaching, and participating in professional organizations, community outreach, publishing, and others.

Quality Assurance: Those planned and systematic actions necessary to provide sufficient confidence that a laboratory's products and services will satisfy quality requirements.

Residency: The tenure of a professional in specialized training, usually occurring after an internship.

Trace Evidence: Any evidence that, because of its size or texture, is easily transferred from one location to another and retained there. Forensic science laboratories may categorize differently what constitutes trace evidence.

Training: Training is the formal, structured process through which a forensic scientist progresses from a current level of scientific knowledge and expertise to the level of competency required to conduct specific forensic analyses.

Appendix A. Forensic Science Careers Outside the Traditional Forensic Science Crime Laboratory

The primary focus of this document is the education and training of individuals working in forensic science laboratories. Careers outside the traditional forensic science laboratory span a wide range of activities, including pathology, engineering, anthropology, and others. Interested students should realize that in some of these fields, the total number of practicing forensic scientists is quite small, and career opportunities may be limited. In some cases, professionals function as part-time forensic science consultants. Most fields can be approached with an undergraduate degree in natural science followed by a forensic-based graduate program (e.g., an entomology degree followed by a graduate forensic entomology program).

Students are advised to discuss possible career paths with established professionals in the field. Examples of forensic science careers outside traditional forensic science laboratories are described below. This list is not all inclusive, and the interested student may investigate other possible career areas in forensic science.

Forensic Pathology

Forensic pathologists are medical doctors who serve as medical examiners and sometimes as coroners. They determine the cause and manner of death through autopsies and death investigation. They are licensed physicians who have completed medical school, 5 years of pathology internship and residency, and 1 year of forensic pathology fellowship. They have passed general medical certification exams as well as pathology (anatomic pathology and/or clinical pathology) and forensic pathology board examinations administered by the American Board of Pathology. The principal professional organization is the National Association of Medical Examiners (http://www.thename.org).

Forensic Psychiatry

Forensic psychiatrists are medical doctors who serve as researchers and clinical practitioners in the many areas in which psychiatry is applied to legal issues. They conduct psychiatric evaluations to determine civil and criminal competence, psychological trauma, criminal responsibility, etc. Forensic psychiatrists may serve prison systems and mental hospitals and act as consultants to prosecutors and criminal defense attorneys. They are licensed physicians who have completed medical school and 4 years in psychiatry internship and residency and have received training in forensic psychiatry. They have passed general medical certification exams and psychiatry board examinations administered by the American Board of Psychiatry and Neurology (http://www.abpn.com). The principal professional organization is the American Academy of Psychiatry and the Law (http://www.emory.edu/AAPL).

Forensic Psychology

Forensic psychology applies the science and profession of psychology to questions and issues relating to the law and the legal system. Forensic psychology includes psychological evaluation and expert testimony regarding such criminal forensic issues as trial competency, forensic behavioral analysis, civil commitment and guardianship, and others. Forensic psychologists must obtain a graduate degree, be licensed by a State board, and may be board certified by the American Board of Professional Psychology (ABPP) (http://www.abpp.org). The American Academy of Forensic Psychology (AAFP) is the education and training arm of the American Board of Forensic Psychology (ABFP) (http://www.abfp.com), which is responsible for board certifications in forensic psychology. Both AAFP and ABFP are part of the ABPP.

Forensic Nursing

Forensic nurses perform a wide range of functions, including serving as sexual assault nurse examiners (SANEs) and case reviewers for medical malpractice attorneys. Forensic nurses are typically registered nurses, and some have bachelor of science degrees in nursing or graduate degrees. Many nursing educational programs now have specific forensic nursing curriculums. The principal professional organization is the International Association of Forensic Nurses (http://www.forensicnurse.org).

Forensic Engineering

In addition to the usual categories of engineering, engineering sciences include physics, chemistry, geophysics, etc. The forensic work of individuals in these fields is most often related to civil litigation, although occasionally their skills are needed in criminal casework. Forensic engineers usually have engineering degrees and, in the United States, are often registered professional engineers. Alternatively, scientists engaged in this work often have doctorates in their respective fields. The range of forensic activity in the engineering sciences includes accident reconstructions, product failure investigations, structural failure analysis, and related investigations. The American Academy of Forensic Sciences (AAFS) (http://www.aafs.org) has an engineering sciences section. Certification in the forensic engineering sciences is available from the International Institute of Forensic Engineering Sciences.

Forensic Anthropology

Forensic anthropologists are physical anthropologists who generate biological profiles (sex, age, height, etc.) for unidentified human skeletal remains, identify unknown individuals, and evaluate skeletal trauma. Forensic anthropologists are often university based and consult for medical examiner offices, although some are employed directly by medical examiner offices. They have graduate degrees in physical or forensic anthropology and may be certified by the American Board of Forensic Anthropology. The largest group of forensic anthropologists works for the military in the U.S. Army's Central Identification Laboratory–Hawaii [Now the Joint POW/MIA Accounting Command] (http://www. cilhi.army.mil). The principal professional organizations are AAFS, Forensic Anthropology Section, and the American Association of Physical Anthropology (http://www.physanth.org).

Forensic Entomology

Forensic entomologists are often university based and consult for medical examiners, coroners, law enforcement agencies, and attorneys. They use insect evidence to help reconstruct the circumstances (e.g., time of death, movement of the body) surrounding human death. Most are Ph.D. entomologists who have become board certified in forensic entomology by the American Board of Forensic Entomology (http://www.missouri.edu/~aqwww/entomology). The principal professional organizations are AAFS and the

Entomological Society of America (http://www.entsoc.org).

Forensic Odontology

Forensic odontologists are dentists and oral pathologists who most often consult for medical examiner offices; few are employed full time by medical examiner offices. They identify people from dental structures and analysis/comparisons of bitemarks. They have received a D.D.S., D.M.D., or equivalent degree and been certified in forensic odontology by the American Board of Forensic Odontology. The principal professional organization is AAFS, Forensic Odontology Section.

Forensic Computer Science/Digital Evidence

Forensic computer specialists are computer and information scientists/technicians who may be involved in the recovery and examination of probative information from digital evidence. The types of evidence include both hardware (desktop computers, laptop computers, network servers, and other digital equipment including cameras, personal digital assistants, pagers, software programs, databases, electronic mail, etc.). The discipline of forensic computer science is, by comparison with the other forensic disciplines listed in this appendix, relatively new, and many areas of the field are not yet defined. Useful sources for information about forensic computer science are the National White Collar Crime Center (http://www.nw3c.org) and the Scientific Working Group on Digital Evidence (SWGDE) (http://www.swgde.org).

Forensic Toxicology

Forensic toxicologists are scientists who provide services in postmortem cases (support death investigations), human performance cases (driving under the influence of alcohol and/or drugs) and workplace testing (mandatory job-related alcohol/drug testing). Although some toxicologists work within the criminalistics/crime laboratory structure, most work in other government and private laboratories. B.S., M.S., and Ph.D. degrees are common. The work, which encompasses the determination and interpretation of drugs and their metabolites in biological fluids, requires significant training in chemistry, biology, physiology, and pharmacology. The principal membership organizations are the Society of Forensic Toxicologists (http://www.soft-tox.org) and the Toxicology Section of AAFS. Many toxicologists are certified by the American Board of Forensic Toxicology as Diplomates or Forensic Toxicology Certification Board Specialists.

Appendix B. Non-TWGED Reviewers

C.G.G. Aitken
The University of Edinburgh
Department of Mathematics and Statistics
The King's Buildings
Edinburgh, Scotland, UK EH9 3JZ
cgga@maths.ed.ac.uk

Sanford Angelos
Senior Forensic Chemist
U.S. Department of Justice
536 South Clark Street
Suite 800
Chicago, IL 60605
forensicchem@21century.net

Sevil Atasoy
Director
Institute of Forensic Science
Istanbul University
Adli Tip Enstitus
34303 Cerrahpasa
Istanbul, Turkey
atasoy@turk.net

Suzanne Bell
Eastern Washington University
Department of Chemistry
226 Science Building
Cheney, WA 99004
suzanne.bell@mail.ewu.edu

Robert Bost
Director
Master of Science in Forensic Science Program
University of Central Oklahoma
Department of Chemistry
Edmond, OK 73034

JoAnn Buscaglia
FBI Academy
Forensic Science Research Unit
Quantico, VA 22135
jbuscaglia@fbiacademy.edu

Charles Cornett
University of Wisconsin–Platteville
Department of Chemistry and Engineering Physics
One University Plaza
Platteville, WI 53818

W. Raymond Cummins
Director
Program in Forensic Science
University of Toronto
3359 Mississauga Road
Toronto, Ontario, Canada L5L 1C6
raymond.cummins@utoronto.ca

Harold Deadman
Department of Forensic Sciences
The George Washington University
Washington, DC 20052

Hiram Evans
Adjunct Professor
California State University–Los Angeles
San Bernardino County Sheriff's Department Laboratory
9500 Etiwanda Avenue
Rancho Cucamonga, CA 91729-6979
hiramevans@compuserve.com

Ken Furton
Director
Forensic Science Programs
Florida International University
Miami, FL 33199
furton@fiu.edu

Brian Gestring
New York City Office of Chief Medical Examiner
520 First Avenue
New York City, NY 10016

David Gibo
Associate Professor of Zoology
University of Toronto
3359 Mississauga Road
Mississauga, Ontario, Canada L5L 1C

Dennis Hilliard
Director
Rhode Island State Crime Laboratory
University of Rhode Island
220 Fogarty Hall-URI
41 Lower College Road
Kingston, RI 02881
dch@uri.edu

Patricia Huck
International Criminal Investigative
Training Assistance Program (ICITAP)
U.S. Department of Justice
1331 F Street NW, #500
Washington, DC 20004

Tom Johnson
Dean
School of Public Safety and Professional
Studies
University of New Haven
300 Orange Avenue
West Haven, CT 06516
tataj@charger.newhaven.ct

Lawrence Kaplan
Professor of Chemistry
Williams College
Chemistry Department
Williamstown, MA 01267
lkaplan@williams.edu

Lawrence Kobilinsky
Associate Provost
John Jay College of Criminal Justice
899 Tenth Avenue
New York City, NY 10019
lkjjj@cunyvm.cuny.edu

Susan Land
5304 South Broadway Circle
#3206
Englewood, CO 80110
sland@ci.arvada.co.us

Karl Larsen
Illinois State Police
Forensic Science Center
larsena@isp.state.il.us

Gary Laughlin
McCrone Research Institute
2820 South Michigan Avenue
Chicago, IL 60616

Richard Li
Program Coordinator
College of Criminal Justice
Sam Houston State University
Criminal Justice Center
C–207
Huntsville, TX 77341–2296
cjc_rcl@shsu.edu

Charles Lindqosf
University of Alabama at Birmingham
Department of Criminal Justice
Birmingham, AL 35294
clindqui@sbs.sbs.vab.edu

Ray Liu
Director
Graduate Program in Forensic Science
University of Alabama at Birmingham
901 15th Street South
Birmingham, AL 35294–2060
rliu@sbs.sbs.uab.edu

Bruce McCord
Associate Professor
Ohio University
Department of Chemistry and
Biochemistry
136 Clippinger Laboratories
Athens, OH 45701–2979
mccord@ohiou.edu

Jerry Melbye
Director
Forensic Science Program
University of Toronto
3359 Mississauga Road
Mississauga, Ontario, Canada L5L 1C6
melbye@credit.erin.utoronto.ca

Marilyn Miller
University of New Haven
Forensic Science Department
300 Orange Avenue
West Haven, CT 06516
mtm01_13@charger.newhaven.edu

Michael Moeller
Department Head
Department of Chemical and Industrial Hygiene
University of Northern Alabama
UNA Box 5021, 129 Wesleyan
Florence, AL 35632

Andre Moenssens
Professor of Law, Emeritus
University of Missouri–Kansas City
5100 Rockhill Road
Kansas City, MO 64110
moenssensa@umkc.edu

Turhon Murad
California State University–Chico
Department of Anthropology
315 Butte Hall
Chico, CA 95929–0400
tmurad@csuchico.edu

Niamh NicDaeid
Strathclyde University
Forensic Science Unit
204 George Street
Glasgow, Scotland, UK G1 1XW
n.nicdaeid@strath.ac.uk

Dale Nute
Florida State University
School of Criminology and Criminal Justice
634 West Call Street
Tallahassee, FL 32306–1127
hdnute@mailer.fsu.edu

David Petersen
Assistant Director
Bureau of Criminal Apprehension
Forensic Science Laboratory
1246 University Avenue
St. Paul, MN 55104–4197
david.b.petersen@state.mn.us

Joseph Peterson
University of Illinois at Chicago
Department of Criminal Justice
1007 West Harrison Street
Chicago, IL 60607
joepete@uic.edu

Lawrence Quarino
Director of Forensic Science
Department of Chemistry
Cedar Crest College
Allentown, PA 18104
lquarino@sprynet.com

Rex Riis
Director
South Dakota Forensic Laboratory
Miller-Matthews Building
3500 East Highway 34
Pierre, SD 57501
rex.riis@state.sd.us

Walter Rowe
Professor of Forensic Science
Department of Forensic Sciences
The George Washington University
Washington, DC 20052
wfrowe@gwis2.circ.gwu.edu

Richard Saferstein
Forensic Science Consultant
20 Forrest Court
Mount Laurel, NJ 08054

Jay Siegel
Professor of Forensic Science
School of Criminal Justice
Michigan State University
506 Baker Hall
East Lansing, MI 48824
Jay.Siegel@ssc.msu.edu

Moses Schanfield
Chair
Department of Forensic Science
The George Washington University
102 Samson Hall
2036 H Street NW
Washington, DC 20052
mschanfield@netscape.net

Fred Smith
Director, Forensic Science Program
University of Alabama–Birmingham
fsmith@uab.edu

James Starrs
Professor of Law and Forensic Science
The George Washington University
720 20th Street, NW
Washington, DC 20052

Steven A. Steiner
Associate Professor
Department of Chemistry and Engineering Physics
University of Wisconsin–Platteville
1 University Plaza
Platteville, WI 53818

David Stoney
McCrone Research Institute
2820 South Michigan Avenue
Chicago, IL 60616
dstoney@mcri.org

Peter Striupaitis
Illinois State Police
striupp@isp.state.il.us

Pat Thiel
Professor of Chemistry
Iowa State University
1605 Gillman Hall
Ames, IA 50011

J.W. Thorpe
Strathclyde University
Forensic Science Unit
204 George Street
Glasgow, Scotland, UK G1 1XW
j.w.thorpe@strath.ac.uk

Appendix C. Forensic Science Professional and Certification Organizations

Professional Organizations

American Academy of Forensic Sciences (AAFS), http://www.aafs.org

American Society of Crime Laboratory Directors (ASCLD), http://www.ascld.org

American Society of Questioned Document Examiners (ASQDE), http://www.asqde.org

Association of Firearms and Tool Mark Examiners (AFTE), http://www.afte.org

Association of Forensic Quality Assurance Managers (AFQAM), http://www.afqam.org

California Association of Criminalists (CAC), http://www.cacnews.org

California Association of Toxicologists (CAT), http://www.cal-tox.org

Clandestine Laboratory Investigating Chemists Association (CLIC)

International Association for Identification (IAI), http://www.theiai.org

Mid-Atlantic Association of Forensic Scientists (MAAFS), http://maafs.org

Midwestern Association of Forensic Scientists (MAFS), http://www.mafs.net

National White Collar Crime Center (NW3C), http://www.nw3c.org

Northeastern Association of Forensic Scientists (NEAFS), http://www.neafs,org

Northwestern Association of Forensic Scientists (NWAFS), http://www.nwafs.org

Society of Forensic Toxicologists (SOFT), http://www.soft-tox.org

Southern Association of Forensic Scientists (SAFS), http://www.southernforensic.org

Southwestern Association of Forensic Scientists (SWAFS), http://www.swafs.us

Certification Organizations

American Board of Criminalists (ABC)[a]

American Board of Forensic Anthropology (ABFA)[b]

American Board of Forensic Document Examiners (ABFDE)[a]

American Board of Forensic Entomology (ABFE)[b]

American Board of Forensic Odontology (ABFO)[a]

American Board of Forensic Toxicology (ABFT)[a]

American Board of Medicolegal Death Investigators (ABMDI)[a]

American Board of Pathology—Forensic Pathology (ABP(FP)[c]

American Board of Psychiatry and Neurology—Forensic Pathology (ABPN–FP)[c]

Association of Firearm and Toolmark Examiners (AFTE)[b]

Association of Forensic Document Examiners (AFDE)[a]

Forensic Toxicologist Certification Board (FTCB)[a]

International Association for Identification (IAI)[a]

International Institute of Forensic Engineering Sciences (IIFES)[a]

Notes

a. Represented on the Forensic Specialties Accreditation Board (FSAB).

b. Recognized as a certification board representing that discipline but not yet formally represented on FSAB.

c. Accredited by the American Board of Medical Specialties.

Appendix D. Technical and Scientific Working Groups

NIJ-Sponsored Technical Working Groups

Technical Working Group for Bombing Scene Investigation (TWGBSI)

Technical Working Group for Crime Scene Investigation (TWGCSI)

Technical Working Group for Death Investigation (TWGDI)

Technical Working Group for Digital Evidence (TWGDE)

Technical Working Group for Eyewitness Evidence (TWGEYEE)

Technical Working Group for Fire/Arson Scene Investigation (TWGFASI)

Technical Working Group for Mass Fatality Forensic Identification (TWGMFFI)

FBI-Sponsored Scientific Working Groups

Scientific Working Group on Bloodstain Pattern Analysis (SWGSTAIN)

Scientific Working Group on Digital Evidence (SWGDE)

Scientific Working Group on DNA Analysis Methods (SWGDAM)

Scientific Working Group on Firearms and Toolmarks (SWGGUN)

Scientific Working Group on Friction Ridge Analysis, Study, and Technology (SWGFAST)

Scientific Working Group on Imaging Technologies (SWGIT)

Scientific Working Group on Materials Analysis (SWGMAT)

Scientific Working Group on Microbial Genetics and Forensics (SWGMGF)

Scientific Working Group on Forensic Document Examination (SWGDOC)

DEA-Sponsored Working Group

Scientific Working Group for the Analysis of Seized Drugs (SWGDRUG)

National Center for Forensic Science-Sponsored Working Group

Technical Working Group for Fire and Explosions Investigations (TWGFEX)

Appendix E. Technical and Scientific Working Groups' Educational Criteria

Scientific Working Group on DNA Analysis Methods (SWGDAM), "Training Guidelines," *Forensic Science Communications* 3(4), 2001, http://www.fbi.gov/hq/lab/fsc/backissu/oct2001/kzinski.htm.

Scientific Working Group on Imaging Technologies (SWGIT), "Guidelines and Recommendations for Training in Imaging Technologies in the Criminal Justice System," *Forensic Science Communications* 4(2), 2002, http://www.fbi.gov/hq/lab/fsc/backissu/april2002/swgittraining.htm.

Scientific Working Group on Materials Analysis (SWGMAT), "Trace Evidence Quality Assurance Guidelines," *Forensic Science Communications* 2(1), 2000, http://www.fbi.gov/hq/lab/fsc/backissu.jan2000/swgmat.htm.

About the National Institute of Justice

NIJ is the research, development, and evaluation agency of the U.S. Department of Justice. The Institute provides objective, independent, evidence-based knowledge and tools to enhance the administration of justice and public safety. NIJ's principal authorities are derived from the Omnibus Crime Control and Safe Streets Act of 1968, as amended (see 42 U.S.C. §§ 3721–3723).

The NIJ Director is appointed by the President and confirmed by the Senate. The Director establishes the Institute's objectives, guided by the priorities of the Office of Justice Programs, the U.S. Department of Justice, and the needs of the field. The Institute actively solicits the views of criminal justice and other professionals and researchers to inform its search for the knowledge and tools to guide policy and practice.

Strategic Goals

NIJ has seven strategic goals grouped into three categories:

Creating relevant knowledge and tools

1. Partner with State and local practitioners and policymakers to identify social science research and technology needs.
2. Create scientific, relevant, and reliable knowledge—with a particular emphasis on terrorism, violent crime, drugs and crime, cost-effectiveness, and community-based efforts—to enhance the administration of justice and public safety.
3. Develop affordable and effective tools and technologies to enhance the administration of justice and public safety.

Dissemination

4. Disseminate relevant knowledge and information to practitioners and policymakers in an understandable, timely, and concise manner.
5. Act as an honest broker to identify the information, tools, and technologies that respond to the needs of stakeholders.

Agency management

6. Practice fairness and openness in the research and development process.
7. Ensure professionalism, excellence, accountability, cost-effectiveness, and integrity in the management and conduct of NIJ activities and programs.

Program Areas

In addressing these strategic challenges, the Institute is involved in the following program areas: crime control and prevention, including policing; drugs and crime; justice systems and offender behavior, including corrections; violence and victimization; communications and information technologies; critical incident response; investigative and forensic sciences, including DNA; less-than-lethal technologies; officer protection; education and training technologies; testing and standards; technology assistance to law enforcement and corrections agencies; field testing of promising programs; and international crime control.

In addition to sponsoring research and development and technology assistance, NIJ evaluates programs, policies, and technologies. NIJ communicates its research and evaluation findings through conferences and print and electronic media.

To find out more about the National Institute of Justice, please visit:

http://www.ojp.usdoj.gov/nij

or contact:

National Criminal Justice
Reference Service
P.O. Box 6000
Rockville, MD 20849–6000
800–851–3420
e-mail: *askncjrs@ncjrs.org*

www.ingramcontent.com/pod-product-compliance
Lightning Source LLC
Chambersburg PA
CBHW080543290526
45790CB00006B/2524

9781502800183